TRACK AND FIELD

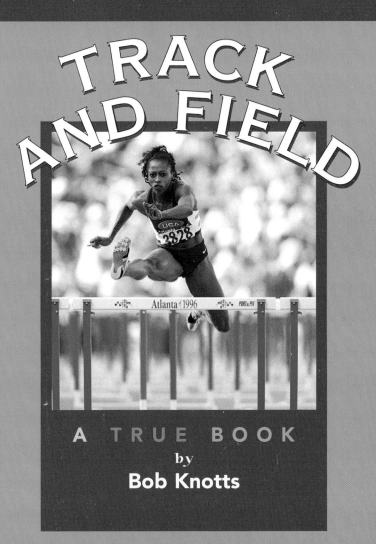

Atlanta 1996

A TRUE BOOK

by
Bob Knotts

Children's Press®
A Division of Grolier Publishing

New York London Hong Kong Sydney
Danbury, Connecticut

The high jump

Reading Consultant
Linda Cornwell
*Coordinator of School Quality
and Professional Improvement
Indiana State Teachers
Association*

Author's Dedication:
*Again to Jill—and to my
parents, Bill and Jeanette.*

Visit Children's Press® on
the Internet at:
http://publishing.grolier.com

Library of Congress Cataloging-in-Publication Data

Knotts, Bob.
    Track and field / by Bob Knotts.
        p.   cm. — (True book)
    Includes bibliographical references and index.
    Summary: Describes the history of track competitions and the various
events involved, as well as several of the stars in the sport.
    ISBN 0-516-21066-1 (lib. bdg.)   0-516-27031-1 (pbk.)
    1. Track-athletics Juvenile literature.   2. Track and field athletics
Juvenile literature. [1. Track and Field.] I. Title. II. Series.
GV1060.5.K57 2000
796.42—dc21   99-15088
                                                                          CIP
                                                                          AC

GROLIER
PUBLISHING

Contents

Run Fast, Jump High, Throw Far

People have always run fast. Long ago, they ran fast to catch food. They probably ran even faster to escape wild animals or enemies. But there was another reason that people ran fast in ancient times. They ran because people like to run.

Track is a sport for people who love to run.

People still like to run. It feels good to move fast on your legs. You feel the wind blowing through your hair. You see and hear and smell interesting things. Running can be fun!

Some people like to run so much that they do it as a sport. The sport of running is called track. This is because the athletes run on an oval track. The track is usually 400 meters long and wide enough for many

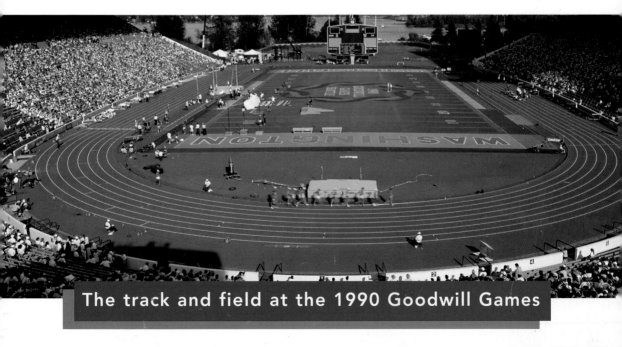

runners to start at the same time. Each runner starts in his or her own part of the track, called a lane.

The runners must run around turns if the race is more than 100 meters long. To make the race fair when this happens, the runners start from different places. Outside lanes are a little longer than inside lanes on an oval track. So runners in outside lanes get a head start.

The start of a men's
400-meter race

At track competitions, called
track meets, runners compete
in different types of races.
Some races are short sprints
that require great speed. Other
races are very long and require
the athletes to run hard for

9

Some races, such as the 200 meters (left), are short sprints, while others, such as the marathon (right), are very long.

hours. Still other races are in-between distances that require both speed and energy.

But some events at a track meet don't require much running. They are called field events because they take place

In the shot put, an athlete spins around and throws a heavy ball as far as possible.

on a large playing field inside the track. Some competitors in these events throw things long distances. Others jump very high or very far. One field event is called the pole vault. Athletes use a long, flexible pole to help hoist themselves

The pole vault

over a tall bar. The pole vault requires strength and skill.

Athletes have competed in track-and-field events for centuries. Track and field was even part of the Olympic Games in ancient Greece.

The Biggest Track Meet of All

A men's relay race during the 1996 Atlanta Olympics

Every four years, the world's best track-and-field athletes compete in the Summer Olympic Games. The Olympics are the most important competition in track and field—and in many other sports.

This was also true in ancient Greece, where the Olympics started. The only event at the first Olympics was a footrace of about 180 meters. In time, more events were added

A discus-throw competition during the ancient Olympic Games

to the Olympics, including many other track-and-field events.

The Sprint Races

A very short footrace is called a sprint. Sprints don't last long. A gun is fired in the air and the runners dash off at top speed. They never slow down until they pass the finish line.

The shortest race is the 100-meter race. The winner

Short footraces are called sprints.

of the men's 100 meters is called the "world's fastest human," and the runners get faster every year. In 1896, the first Olympic winner finished

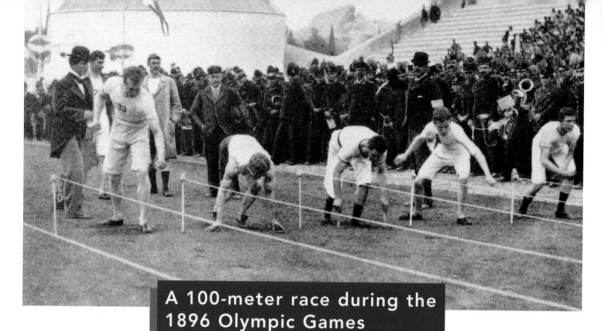

A 100-meter race during the 1896 Olympic Games

this race in 12 seconds. Today, the best sprinters finish in less than 10 seconds.

Sprinters also compete in the 200-meter, 400-meter, and 800-meter races. In what is called a relay race, four runners on one team take turns.

Each member of the team races a certain distance and is then replaced by a teammate. The runners must carry a metal tube called a baton. When they finish, they hand the baton to the next runner.

A women's 4x100-meter relay race

A hurdler must jump at just the right moment to clear the hurdle.

Some sprinters even jump over things during their races. These athletes run at top speed and leap over hurdles, which are like high gates. They must jump at just the right instant as they run—not too soon or too late. This takes lots of practice.

The Long Races

Many runners compete in longer races. These athletes must run for a longer time than sprinters, so they can't use up their energy too fast.

The most famous race of all is the longest race—the marathon. Can you imagine running for more than

The marathon is the longest long-distance race.

26 miles (42 km)? Marathon runners race that far. It takes about two hours for the best marathoners to finish.

A women's 5,000-meter race (above) and a 3,000-meter steeplechase (left)

The next-longest races are 5,000 meters and 10,000 meters. There is also a long event called the steeplechase, in which runners jump over hurdles and water during the race.

Roger Bannister was the first person to run a mile in under 4 minutes.

The 1,500 meters, which is almost 1 mile long, is also a famous race. For many years, people thought no one could run a mile in less than 4 minutes. But in 1954, a British runner named Roger Bannister proved that they were wrong. He was the first person to do it. Today's runners finish this race in about 3 1/2 minutes.

Probably the oddest-looking races to watch are the walking events. Race walkers wiggle

A race walker

their hips while walking as fast as their legs can move. But these races are very tiring. Men race in the 20,000-meter and 50,000-meter walks. Women race in the 10,000-meter walk.

Field Events

How far can you throw? How far can you jump? How high can you jump? This is what field athletes try to find out each time they compete.

All field events require great strength. Two of these events are the discus throw and the hammer throw. The

The discus throw

discus is a round disk that looks like a small flying saucer. The hammer is a metal ball attached to a wire and handle.

The hammer throw

The athlete spins around
before throwing the discus or
hammer as far as possible.
The longest throw wins.

The javelin throw

The longest throw also wins
in two other events—the javelin
and shot put. The javelin is a
long spear that athletes throw
after running a few steps. In the

shot put, competitors spin around and then toss a heavy metal ball. It takes years of training to be the best in the javelin or shot put—or in any other field event.

The shot put

Several different jumping events are included in field events. In the pole vault, for example, athletes use a long, flexible pole to help hoist themselves over a tall bar. The winning athlete is the one who can go over the highest bar without knocking it down.

In the high jump, competitors use only their legs to jump over a tall bar. The athletes run before jumping off from one foot. They use

The winner of the high jump (above) is the one who leaps over the highest bar without knocking it down. A pole vaulter lifts up on her pole (left).

speed, strength, and skill to get over the bar without knocking it down.

Long jumper Bob Beamon during the 1968 Olympics

The only thing that matters in the long jump is how far you jump. Competitors run fast to a board placed in the ground. Then they push off into the air. They may swing their arms and legs forward to get more distance. During the 1968 Olympics, American athlete Bob Beamon amazed the world with a jump of more than 29 feet (9 m).

The triple jump is an unusual event. The athletes start by running and jumping into the air, just as they do in the long jump. But then they land on one foot and hop onto the other foot. Then they quickly jump again. This event used to

An athlete sailing through the air during the triple jump

be called the "hop, step, and jump." It sometimes looks strange to watch—but it's hard to do.

The Decathlon and the Heptathlon

Two of the hardest track-and-field sports require many different skills. Men compete in the decathlon, which has ten track-and-field events. Women take part in the heptathlon, which has seven track-and-field events.

To win, both men and women must do everything well—run fast, jump high and far, and throw things a long way. The Olympic decathlon winner is called the "world's greatest athlete."

Great Britain's Daley Thompson won two Olympic decathlons.

A heptathlon competitor

Great Track-and-Field Champions

One of the first modern track-and-field champions was Jim Thorpe. He was a Native American born in 1886 and a great athlete in many sports.

In the 1912 Olympics, Thorpe won two gold medals. He won the decathlon and a

Jim Thorpe throwing the discus during the 1912 Olympic pentathlon five-event track-and-field sport called the pentathlon. The pentathlon was later dropped from track competitions.

This is how great Thorpe was—his decathlon scores in the 1912 Olympics would have won second place in the 1948 Olympics!

Finland's Paavo Nurmi was the greatest track star of the 1920s. He carried a stopwatch when he ran so that he could regulate his pace. Known as

Finland's Paavo Nurmi won six gold medals in three Olympics in the 1920s.

the "Flying Finn," Nurmi won nine medals in three Olympics, including six gold medals.

Babe Didrikson won the javelin throw in the 1932 Olympics.

A great woman champion was American Babe Didrikson. She won the javelin throw and the 80-meter hurdles in the 1932 Olympics. She came in second in the high jump during the same Olympics. Later, Didrikson became a great golfer. She was voted the Greatest Woman Athlete of the first half of the twentieth century.

Carl Lewis is sometimes called the "Greatest Olympian Ever." This American track-and-field

Carl Lewis (center) celebrating victory at the 1996 Olympics

star won nine Olympic gold medals. Lewis was great in sprint races and in the long jump. He was the first man to win the title "world's fastest human" in two Olympics.

Do you think you might become an Olympic champion someday? Do you love to run and throw and jump? You will have to practice hard for many years just to make an Olympic team. But if you love track and field, you might have lots of fun trying!

The start of a junior 1,000-meter race

To Find Out More

Here are some additional resources to help you learn more about track and field:

 **Books**

Hunter, Shaun. **Great African Americans in the Olympics.** Crabtree Publications, 1997.

Perry, Philippa. **Olympic Gold.** World Book, 1996.

Plowden, Martha Ward. **Olympic Black Women.** Pelican Publishing, 1995.

Sandelson, Robert. **Track Athletes** (Olympic Sports). Crestwood House, 1991.

Wallechinsky, David. **The Complete Book of the Summer Olympics.** Little, Brown & Co., 1996.

Organizations and Online Sites

International Amateur Athletic Federation (IAAF)
http://www.iaaf.org

Find out about the organization that supervises all international track meets.

International Olympic Committee (IOC)
http://www.olympic.org

This page can tell you about the organization that runs all Olympic Games.

Pan American Games Organizing Committee
Pan American
Games Society
500 Shaftesbury Blvd.
Winnipeg, Manitoba
R3P 0M1 Canada

The Pan American Games include one of the most important track meets other than the Olympics.

United States Olympic Committee (USOC)
Olympic House
One Olympic Plaza
Colorado Springs, CO
80909-5760
http://www.usoc.org

The United States Olympic Committee supervises Olympic activity for the United States. Its website includes everything you want to know about Olympic sports, past and present.

USA Track & Field
P.O. Box 120
One RCA Dome, Ste. 140
Indianapolis, IN
46206-0120
http://www.usatf.org/

USA Track & Field supervises track and field events for United States athletes. Its website includes profiles of U.S. track-and-field stars, past and present.

Important Words

baton light wooden or metal tube used in relay races

decathlon men's track-and-field competition that has ten events, including short and long runs, jumping, and throwing

flexible easily bended

heptathlon women's track-and-field competition that has seven events, including short runs, jumping, and throwing

hurdles high gates that runners must jump over at high speed

relay race track event in which four athletes on one team take turns running while carrying a baton

sprint very short footrace on foot that requires great speed

steeplechase race during which runners jump over hurdles and water jumps

Index

Meet the Author

Bob Knotts is the author of five True Books on Summer Olympic sports. He also writes for national magazines, including *Sports Illustrated*, *Reader's Digest*, *Family Circle*, *Travel & Leisure*, and *USA Weekend*. He has worked as a newspaper reporter as well as in radio and television. He has been nominated twice for the Pulitzer Prize. Mr. Knotts resides with his wife, Jill, near Fort Lauderdale, Florida.